Ruby & Begonia's
Christmas Style

Sara Toliver
& Jo Packham

Sterling Publishing Co., Inc. New York
A Sterling/Chapelle Book

Chapelle, Ltd.:
  Jo Packham
  Sara Toliver
  Cindy Stoeckl

  Editor: Lecia Monsen
  Editorial Director: Caroll Shreeve
  Art Director: Karla Haberstich
  Graphic Illustrator: Kim Taylor
  Copy Editor: Marilyn Goff
  Staff: Burgundy Alleman, Areta Bingham, Ray Cornia,
  Emily Frandsen, Marilyn Goff, Lana Hall, Susan
  Jorgensen, Barbara Milburn, Karmen Quinney, Suzy
  Skadburg, Desirée Wybrow

If you have any questions or comments, please contact:
Chapelle, Ltd., Inc., P.O. Box 9252, Ogden, UT 84409
(801) 621-2777 • (801) 621-2788 Fax
e-mail: chapelle@chapelleltd.com
web site: www.chapelleltd.com

The copy, photographs, instructions, illustrations, and designs in this
volume are intended for the personal use of the reader and may be
reproduced for that purpose only. Any other use, especially commercial use,
is forbidden under law without the written permission of the copyright holder.

Every effort has been made to ensure that all information in this book is
accurate. However, due to differing conditions, tools, and individual skills,
the publisher cannot be responsible for any injuries, losses, and/or other
damages which may result from the use of the information in this book.

This volume stimulates decorating ideas. If readers are unfamiliar or not
proficient in a skill necessary to attempt a project, we urge that they
refer to an instructional book specifically addressing the required technique.

Library of Congress Cataloging-in-Publication

  Ruby & Begonia's Christmas style / Sara Toliver & Jo Packham.
     p. cm.
  "A Sterling/Chapelle book."
  Includes index.
  ISBN 1-4027-0110-1
  1. Christmas decorations—United States. 2. Interior
decorations—United States. I. Packham, Jo. II. Title.
TT900.C4T65 2003
394.2663—dc21
                              2003005846

10 9 8 7 6 5 4 3 2 1

Published in paperback 2004 by Sterling Publishing Co., Inc.
387 Park Avenue South, New York, NY 10016
©2003 by Sara Toliver and Jo Packham
Distributed in Canada by Sterling Publishing
c/o Canadian Manda Group, One Atlantic Avenue, Suite 105
Toronto, Ontario, Canada M6K 3E7
Distributed in Great Britain by Chrysalis Books Group PLC
The Chrysalis Building, Bramley Road, London W10 6SP, England
Distributed in Australia by Capricorn Link (Australia) Pty. Ltd.
P. O. Box 704, Windsor, NSW 2756, Australia
Printed and Bound in China
All Rights Reserved

Sterling ISBN 1-4027-0110-1 Hardcover
            ISBN 1-4027-1769-5 Paperback

Introduction

Whether celebrated on a ranch on the open range, in a cabin in the middle of the Northwoods, or at a chalet in the aspen hills, the holiday season of Christmas is a special time of year filled with the anticipation, wonder, and joy that is inherent in such a memorable occasion. It is not a celebration that must be postcard perfect or taken directly from the pages of a Dicken's novel. It is the one time of the year that, through its timeless and simple traditions, opens up our hearts, brings cause to reflect and rejoice, and offers to each of us a quiet blessing of peace. It is a time when we do what we would not ordinarily do in the early days of spring or the long days of summer. We decorate our homes extravagantly, prepare large feasts, and host wondrous parties. It is, for many, the time of year that offers much and in which memories are more precious than those of any other season.

In our homes and at our shop, *Ruby & Begonia*, both Sara and I believe that "an embarrassment of riches" brings a joy that is necessary at least once during the year. What better time than a season of thanksgiving, rejoicing, and gift giving? Regardless of where you live, when you speak of the season of Christmas, you think of new fallen snow, freshly cut pine trees, blazing fires, gifts selected and given from the heart, homes all dressed up in their Christmas finery, and time spent with family and friends. It is this time of year when you drive from house to house and are cheered by the holiday decorations, enter shops and are greeted with hot cider and the scent of cinnamon, return home and are welcomed with the wonder and merriment of small children. During this season, we create a magic that is shared with family, friends, and customers. We do our creative best to make the holiday season all that dreams are made of. We decorate the trees, pay special attention to the wrapping of the packages, help with the planning of parties, assist in the recording of memories, and we share in the true spirit of Christmas built on special traditions while establishing new ones.

We would like to say thank you for sharing with us all of our favorite Christmas ideas and secrets and to offer our Christmas wishes of joy and peace throughout the year.

Sara Toliver and Jo Packham

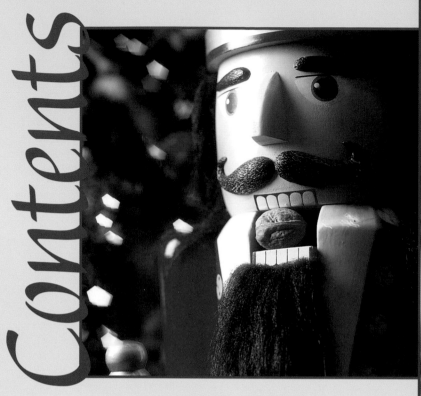

Contents

decorate for a simple country *Christmas*

Regardless of where we live, all of us have a special memory "somewhere" of a "simple country Christmas." A season when snow covers the fence posts and neighbors come to call bringing freshly baked goods and homemade ornaments that were inspired by the simple joys of country living.

An old-fashioned country Christmas celebrates timeless yuletide traditions as they are lived today by families everywhere. The simplicity of country and folk art is created to tell stories of families growing up, attending church, and sharing traditions. Whether we actually lived the stories or just wish we could have, they can be easily re-created.

A simple country Christmas is filled with all that is natural—tiny birds in their nests, wooden snowflakes painted white, miniature churches complete with steeples, handmade dolls, and ornaments created by children. Everything you need for such a celebration is here in this chapter, re-created by us at *Ruby & Begonia* or by you in your own home. All you need to add for an old-fashioned country Christmas is love.

Decorating for the holiday season in the country is simple. To make this a memorable occasion at *Ruby & Begonia,* we gather family and friends together for dinner one evening before Thanksgiving. After dinner everyone congregates around the fireplace or in the kitchen to make garlands and ornaments for the trees. We supply bowls of cranberries, popcorn, dried oranges and apples, nuts, cinnamon dough, cloves and cinnamon sticks, tiny baskets, miniature bird's nests, small pinecones and other natural materials, lots of string, and a small drill with a ¹⁄₁₆" drill bit. As each of us creates our "treasures for the tree," photographs are taken to be placed in small frames that hang from garlands and wreaths throughout our homes and store.

For seasonal decorating, an old fireplace mantel can be placed on a blank wall and used as a focal point for handmade Christmas collections. Empty salvaged frames can be used as backdrops to add emphasis to favored pieces. Even though it is a "pretend" fireplace, at the store we never forget to place a saucer of cookies and a glass of milk on a child's chair for Santa when he comes to visit.

Right: We enjoy a garland of ornaments made by friends from scented cinnamon dough, cookie dough, or modeling clay and hung on the mantel.

Country Snow Folk Ornaments

Make snowman-shaped sugar cookies using a favorite recipe or purchased dough.

Using the handle of a watercolor paintbrush, make 5 indentations for buttons, 5 indentations for smile, and 2 indentations for eyes in each snowman. Make 1 hole in the top of each snowman's head and 1 hole in the hand(s). Bake according to directions and cool for 1 minute.

With food coloring, lightly paint indentations black. With diluted red food coloring, blush snowman's cheeks. Using dusty orange modeling clay, mold a small carrot-shaped nose and attach with corn syrup.

Mold small hearts and stars from modeling clay. Using a toothpick, make holes in shapes for hangers. Let pieces dry.

String 2 clay hearts and 1 star on floss and attach to the hole in the hand(s) or tie the star to a cinnamon stick and attach the stick. Tie a loop of floss through the hole in the top of the head for a hanger.

Cinnamon Dough Ornaments

In a mixing bowl, combine 1 cup ground cinnamon, ¼ cup white glue, and enough water to make a dough consistency, approximately ¾ to 1 cup. Chill, covered for 2 hours. Roll out on a surface sprinkled with cinnamon and cut into desired shapes.

Bake on a cookie sheet in a 200° oven for 2 hours, turning every half hour until dry. Cool completely. Using cinnamon sticks for legs, glue to the back of each ornament.

Embellish with ribbons, cloves, cinnamon sticks, herbs, and dried cranberries.

Above: Painted wooden angels add a heavenly touch.

Right: We create our own small wooden ornaments by cutting shapes of familiar images or buying precut wooden pieces from our local craft store.

To make simple country ornaments, three sizes of hearts or stars are layered together with wood glue and distressed with white paint. The same small shape in rusted metal is nailed to the center with a special tack like the ones being used in designer stores for bulletin boards. To distress the ornaments, lightly sand them after they have been painted and allowed to dry.

Metal filigree pieces are added to snowflakes and hearts before white latex-coated wire is bent and affixed through a small drilled hole in the top of each ornament.

14

Christmas Stocking Ornaments

Purchase fabric Christmas stockings or make small stockings from blue-and-white toweling. Write favorite holiday quotes or sayings on the front of the stocking with a dressmaker's pen. Embroider a simple backstitch for the letters and a lazy daisy stitch for flowers and leaves.

Left and below: Try using paint pens or dimensional paints as well as sequins, buttons, and ribbons for embellishing stockings or these snowman ornaments.

The best pictures are kept in the mind; the best memories are kept in the heart.
—Unknown

During the holiday season, gingerbread houses are a favorite of almost everyone. This year in our town, one of our local banks created a fund raiser for a local charity. Individuals, small companies, and large corporations were asked to make, or have made, a gingerbread house that could be donated and sold at auction. A party was given at the bank where the gingerbread houses were on display. While guests were mingling, a silent auction was held and bid sheets displayed by each individual house were filled in. The houses were left on display for two days, during which time customers could come into the bank and raise the bids. It was a wonderful event, raising money for a much needed cause, while giving the community an opportunity to both express and view their talents. On these two pages are photographs of the houses that were country in nature. Some are very whimsical while others are more indicative of a true country Christmas.

Ideas for such gingerbread houses can be taken from the illustrations in children's books. When you see a picture of the house you would like to imitate, take it with you to the grocery store and stretch your imagination to substitute edible items for the "real" building materials. This is a project that can be an event for every member of the family and you need not be a good cook or a great "builder" to be successful.

When creating a gingerbread house, the base the house will be sitting on must be sturdy enough to transport it without bending under the weight. Make it large enough to contain the landscape around the house.

Opposite, left, and above: Part of the magic of building gingerbread houses is the completion of the details. Any edible materials can be used decoratively.

recall a vintage *Christmas*

A vintage-style Christmas at *Ruby & Begonia* is a celebration filled with inspirations of things past, reused or re-created to grace your Christmases of today. A vintage style is one that enjoys the "very pretty" things in life. It displays handwork that was made not only to grace the homes of the very rich but those that were created as beautiful necessities in a working-class household. A vintage style appreciates the faded fabrics that proudly display the years of use. It does not matter if the china used to serve Christmas dinner has a tiny chip or a small crack; because these are proof that, then as now, these items were part of creating memories. A vintage-style Christmas is a re-creation of what is cherished and used, and is for some an important part of much-loved holiday traditions.

"Odd" collections of family treasures are typical of vintage seasonal displays. Santas that were collected on family outings, a grandmother's delicate teacup and pot which she used only on Christmas morning, vintage candlesticks decorated with crystals from an old chandelier, and a variety of antique frames with family photographs are all placed on the mantel with hand-embroidered linens. Notice in the picture, above, that the painting is only set on the mantel, not hung, so it becomes a backdrop to frame the collection and not a piece intended to be noticed singly.

Above: During the holidays, Sara and I often make some of our favorite figurines look more festive and more vintage by adding small objects, pieces of fabric, or by covering them with glitter.

When decorating a special table for the holidays, whether it be for 2 or 20, we will often create our own linens or table coverings. Because we change our store displays with each new month, it is important that we are creative in our use and reuse of materials. One of our designers, Anita Louise Crane, taught us one of her many designer secrets for reusing fabric. If fabric yardage is used in November for window displays, then in December it can be cut into squares that are place-mat size and the edges frayed for our holiday tables. In January we can use the same squares to make book covers.

In a vintage-style Christmas, small details are important. We make garlands in shorter lengths of multiple strands attached at both ends with jewelry findings, similar to necklaces. The strands are beaded with antique beads in nontraditional Christmas colors. Vintage velvet flowers taken from old hats are tied together in small bouquets and attached to the tree limbs. Enamel jeweled frames are filled with family photographs of generations past, and all are placed on rich velvet shawls or throws.

With vintage, Sara and I often add just a touch of something created by artisans of today so the look is not "too yesterday." In the store, hammered-copper candlesticks were placed by the tree on the piano. Strings of miniature square mirrored pieces, crystal votive holders, and glass icicles were tied with satin ribbons and hung from small cup hooks placed in the ceiling.

Wreath making is one of the most ancient of crafts and is a significant part of every Christmas holiday. Traditionally, wreaths were made from natural materials and today, as yesterday, they symbolize love, friendship, and even the circle of life itself. In ancient Greece, wreaths of laurel, oak, and olive leaves were bestowed on winners of different events to honor them. Eventually, natural wreaths made from foliage were replaced by wreaths made of gold for emperors and ancient poets. Today, wreaths can be made from any material for any reason. There are, of course, traditional Christmas wreaths made from pine boughs and pinecones or there are more unique wreaths, like the one above, created from pieces of antique silverware. This wreath can be used simply as a silver wreath or to hold Christmas cards received from friends who live far away or photographs of family members from past Christmas celebrations.

Christmas Cards and Button Cookies
Roll cookie dough out to ¼" thickness.

For Cards: Cut dough in envelope shape with a knife. Cut out 1" squares for stamps. Paint address, postmarks, and stamps with thinned egg yolk and paste food coloring. Let color dry between applications. Bake in pre-heated 350° oven. Remove stamps from cookie sheet if they start to brown.

Remove from cookie sheet and cool completely. Using powdered sugar thinned with water to glue-like consistency, attach stamps to letters.

For Buttons: Cut two layers for each button with a biscuit cutter. Use a drinking glass just smaller than biscuit cutter to impress edge of button in top layer. Make four holes in top layer, stack layers together with filling if desired, paint and bake as instructed above in "For Cards." "Stitch" with frosting.

Food, family, and friends—the very heart of the Christmas holidays . . . for Christmas is a time of baking for those you love. It is a time when you can surprise family and friends with gifts from the kitchen or gifts made by hand—gifts given from the heart.

I personally neither bake treats nor send Christmas cards during the holidays, but I do love to buy ready-made sugar-cookie dough and create Christmas treasures for friends who come to visit. The "Christmas cards" above are given to those that I wish I could see more often, and the small button cookies to the right are my gifts to the many friends I have made over the years who create works of art with needle and thread.

Above: Vintage ornaments have become quite collectible and very expensive. For the store display, we re-create them from supplies and materials that are readily available.

"Vintage" Ornaments

To create your own vintage ornaments, purchase traditional inexpensive glass ornaments, remove the ornament cap and insert a straw. Wrap masking tape around straw and neck of ball. Clean ball with glass cleaner. To free hands while working, insert straw handle into a foam brick. Paint desired design on ornament, using either glass or porcelain paints (depending on the desired look). While the design is drying, paint the cap with a darkened gray paint so that it looks aged. You can also paint the entire ornament a different color so that when it is distressed, a second color will show. A third design idea is to paint a design with high-tack craft glue, then sprinkle glue area with embossing powder or fine glitter. If you do not consider yourself an "artist," collect several publications which contain vintage ornaments and use those for your inspiration. After glue or paint is completely dry, lightly sand ornament with very fine sandpaper. When these are hung on the tree, guests are certain to quietly admire your "vintage" collection.

Glass domes are favored by all who love decorating for any season or occasion that calls for a nostalgic touch. In the arrangement below, a bottle-green glass dome was placed on a rusted tin charger. A small vintage juice glass filled with crystal beads, delicate glass-bead flowers, and jeweled frames with favorite photographs were placed underneath. Christmas collectibles or real flowers can also be placed under domes for holiday decorating as another option.

Above: A vintage-style Christmas garland which can be used on trees, wreaths, or hung as swags, can be made by crocheting hand-dyed ribbon. Dying the ribbon can be as simple or complex as desired. Special cold water dyes can be obtained, Rit® dye can be used, or Sara and I simply paint dyable ribbon with different colors of watered-down acrylic paints. We then take lengths of ribbon and crochet them, using a chain stitch and a looped crochet stitch.

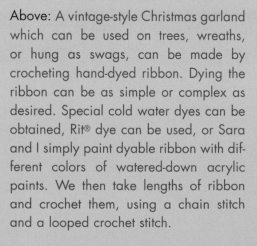

Above: Small handmade fabric hearts were created with pieces of vintage fabrics, beads, and buttons by one of our designers, Dixie Barber. Such tiny re-creations are often more time consuming than they appear, but are as treasured as they are small.

Feather trees have been popular since they were introduced in this country by German immigrants. Today they are created to resemble the originals, which were made from dyed goose or turkey feathers wired to wooden dowels. Their sparse style makes them ideal for displaying intricate ornaments.

Above: The ornaments used on this tree are vintage. However, they can be re-created from new materials as well.

Top left: New ornaments can be made to look vintage with glue and glitter.

Center and bottom left: Sometimes new ornaments are so delicate and so natural as to appear to have been created in another, more genteel time.

Almost any ornament, new or old, can be re-created if desired. The beaded ornaments above can be made by stringing new beads over glass ornaments, painting with glass paint, and then distressing with fine sandpaper. The snowmen are papier-mâché figures, painted white, covered in glitter, and adorned with tiny accents. The pieces of nature are more difficult but are created by coating natural objects in silver, bronze, or copper.

Whether you choose to purchase them or make your own, vintage-style ornaments are sought after by our family, friends, and customers and will be treasured for generations.

A friend showed me a gift that she had received for Christmas and both Sara and I thought it was such a lovely present that we decided to carry it at *Ruby & Begonia*. It is called a "blessings bowl."

During a moment of quiet in your day, sit down and write on a piece of paper one blessing that you have received. Roll the paper into a small scroll, tie it with a ribbon, and place it in the bowl. You do this each day . . . except on the days you are troubled and may have forgotten all of the blessings you enjoy. On those days, instead of writing down a blessing, spend your quiet time reading each scroll to remind yourself of all that you have forgotten or taken for granted. It is a gift that gives back what we sometimes need the most.

Right: The blessings bowl comes beautifully packaged in a purple box, with matching paper fill, and tied with a large organdy bow. The contents are a lovely silver bowl, sheets of vellum paper, tiny pieces of satin ribbon, and a silver pen.

anticipate a child's
Christmas

Christmas and children—what is more natural, more anticipated, or more enjoyed? Whether you have children of your own, grandchildren, nieces, nephews, or young friends, it is a time especially for them and one to be enjoyed with them.

The holiday season with children is a joy that is pure and simple. A time when preparations should be as special as the day itself. Afternoons are to be enjoyed as young ones sit with you to make their own decorations, then participate in the ritual that follows as they help place them on the tree. Pleasure is experienced on Christmas morning when we see the surprise and wonder on their faces as they discover that Santa's reindeer ate the carrots left just for them and that Santa enjoyed each of his cookies and left a note of thanks. We love to hear their squeals of delight as they discover that one special gift Santa left in a special place just for them.

At *Ruby & Begonia*, these traditions and more are those which we help to create and share with all of our younger family members, friends, and patrons.

Some of the patrons that come into our store bring their children and let them select their favorite ornaments from our trees, while others come to gather ideas for creating new memories and ornaments of their own. The projects shown above and below are two of our most popular. The snowmen are made with Styrofoam® balls and tiny black top hats glued on top. The eyes and mouth are buttons and the nose is a small plastic carrot from the craft store. After each is completed, they are painted with white glue and rolled in glitter. The purchased pillow has a tree design of seam binding attached with fabric glue.

Christmas is a time of traditions—celebrated each year just as they were the year before. As my children were growing up, each year they selected their own "child size tree" for their room and decorated it the way they wanted to. Now that they are grown, and their rooms have become guest rooms, I still need my tradition of watching the delight on small faces as they see trees just their size decorated the way they would have decorated them. A family tradition for one of our clients is to buy a new pair of pajamas and make a simple doll, both of which are opened on Christmas Eve. In addition, each year a new needlework piece is completed and given to each of the children by their grandmother.

Right: In the shop we decorate the little one's Christmas tree in white-on-white, pale pink, light blue, and soft yellow.

Right top: At *Ruby & Begonia*, candy canes are made by our smallest patrons by adhering gumdrops to Styrofoam® candy canes. Ice cream cones are made with Styrofoam® balls covered with white glue and rolled in glitter, then glued into real ice cream cones.

Right bottom: Small stuffed toys are ideal ornaments for a young child's tree.

Children love candy whether it is to eat or use in decorating. As the little ones help us decorate trees in the store, they add real candy canes or hard rock candies—usually intended to be swizzle sticks in their parent's coffee. It is a special time when we are able to share in the joys and traditions of all of whom we have come to know throughout the year.

Children, bears, and handmade ornaments are often a tradition for family decorating and each year these families bring out the small treasures that were made by loved ones and friends over the course of many years. On one special evening, one customer prepares a "decorate the tree" dinner and the family gathers around, decorates the tree, and retells the story of each ornament as it is added to the branches by its maker or recipient. These are not the trees that designer's brag about or that you see in the trendiest of decorating magazines, these are the trees that make Christmas a celebration and give holiday decorating its heart and soul.

Left: My dear friend, Holly Bauman, is a collector of teddy bears and one of her most cherished traditions is the decorating of her "teddy bear tree."

Each year Holly hosts a "cousin's party" for her nieces and her grandchildren. Among other weekend activities, each child selects two of the bears from Holly's collection, writes their name and the year on the bear's foot, and places the bear on the tree. As the weekend continues, the bears are taken down, redressed, and oftentimes given a new place of honor on the wooden tree that Holly's husband, Joe, designed and built. It is a wooden tree that resembles a collapsible windmill. When erected, it becomes a solid staircase of spirals for the bears to sit on. Holly wraps a lighted garland around the center of the tree before her young guests arrive.

This year, because the tree is unable to house even one more new bear, the cousins and grandchildren will be able to pick two of their bears to take home as well as select two new bears from Holly's collection to replace them.

Above: Each year during the holidays, the children in this family buy one new Mary Engelbreit® tin for their mother's collection.

Many families traditionally collect a favored series of items. For example, children can give their mother a collectible tin filled with candy each year on Christmas Eve. A picture of the children, taken that year at Christmas, can later be placed inside the tin with a note containing the year and the special happenings of that holiday season.

Above: This version of an older child's nutcracker was made with paper and magic markers.

Below: Dress the youngest ones in their holiday best to be photographed for sweet Christmas memories to come.

37

During the Christmas holidays, children want to be part of the excitement and the preparation. They want to help with the baking, the buying, and the wrapping. While we are busy preparing the store for the holidays, we teach classes so the children of our customers can make ornaments or gifts for their family and friends. These small trains and planes made from a variety of candy and gum are among their favorites.

The train cars are packages of red gum hooked together with a paperclip that is unfolded and bent into an "S" shape. One side of the "S" is glued to the bottom of one package of gum while the other side of the "S" is glued to the connecting "train car". The wheels are hard candy glued to the gum package side and the "freight" can be whatever candy the children choose. We supply cool-glue guns and glue sticks so that the children do not injure themselves with hot glue. We also like to place large bowls of candy on the tables and let the children choose which they will use to make their trains and planes. They know what their friends like and will want to include those in their design.

Children love to wrap packages almost as much as they love to unwrap them. It is a project they enjoy as well as one that will teach them "niceties" that they should know. Everyone likes to receive presents, regardless of how they are wrapped, but when the wrapping is as much fun or as beautiful as the gift, the recipient is doubly delighted. At *Ruby & Begonia*, we are known for the manner in which we wrap our gifts. The color and design of the paper and the ribbons must match the gift that is inside. We would never wrap a pastel-blue baby blanket in dark purple wrap—it is simply not a "Ruby wrap!" We teach our young patrons the same lessons. To us, the presentation of your gift is almost as important as the gift itself. Make it match, make it special, and make it yourself. You will be rewarded with lots of smiles and oohs and ahs.

Above: Create a personalized T-shirt and package it in a canning jar "bug catcher" with screen material under the lid for nature lovers.

Buying presents for children to give is oftentimes expensive and can be frustrating for both the adult and the child. At *Ruby & Begonia* we like to help our younger customers make their own presents. A plain white T-shirt can be rubber stamped, have an iron-on decal applied, or be hand-painted. After the children have selected their method and their artwork, we help them create their gifts. Once completed, these are the gifts they enjoy sharing the most and they are the ones that are the most fun to receive.

gild your home for *Christmas*

The Three Wisemen of old were dressed in robes of the richest velvet and adorned with the most expensive of embellishments. They came offering the gifts of gold, frankincense, and myrrh in jeweled and gilded boxes. This is the lavish style of Christmas, one that is both made and given from the heart, but represents all that is precious, extravagant, glittering, and of great wealth.

At *Ruby & Begonia*, this is the Christmas style that we love the most—that which reiterates our theme of "an embarrassment of riches." We trim the trees with an abundance of ornaments that glitter with gold, sparkle like crystal, or gleam with silver. We fill the store with not only the most splendid sights of Christmas but the most aromatic of fragrances and the stirring chords of music as well. Whenever you enter, candles are always burning and music resounds in every corner. It is this which, for a moment, makes us feel pampered, dignified, and even a little royal.

Above: An elaborate centerpiece, this arrangement of garlands, ornaments, and lights appears to be a small Christmas tree, hung upside down in a wonderfully unusual buffet-style table.

At *Ruby & Begonia*, decorations emulate the stately households of times past. Christmas Eve was traditionally the time reserved for the holiday dinner. It was a quieter, more dignified time when the children were more "subdued" and "manageable" than on Christmas day. The silver was polished, the finest of china was brought from the cupboards, and the imported crystal was placed in its proper position. Today, the "candles" must be lit and the centerpiece must be very grand. The flowers are always fresh, the crystal is handblown, and the music is composed of symphonies and sung by choirs.

To look expensive does not always mean that it was expensive. One secret of designers, when they decorate their own homes, is to incorporate one or two truly magnificent pieces with those that were purchased at after-Christmas sales or from one of the myriad discount stores across the country. Red glass plates, like the ones to the right, can be purchased almost anywhere for a minimal price. The candlesticks and the crystal punch bowl were closeouts at a factory outlet store. Only the cake pedestal is vintage and collectible.

Left: An elegantly decorated home's collection of candlesticks can be placed on a mantelpiece.

As with any collection, it can be built one candlestick at a time and displayed in the center of the dining-room table, on a piano, or on the mantelpiece. Candlesticks can be gifts from family and friends or collected on your business trips or vacations.

43

The traditional color of red and the familiar sight of Santa's boots were what our clients used to decorate with when their children were young. However, now that the children are gone, these are not images that conjure up extravagant decorating. We accented the traditional and the familiar with a tree heavily flocked in snow, hanging crystal ornaments, and deep red hydrangeas, the illusion was immediately re-created. We even encourage our customers to use their heavy metal garden decor in the wintertime by placing it under the tree. Rusted candlesticks can be painted white, then distressed. Metal flowerpots are stacked and filled with winter berries. Even Santa's boots could receive a new coat of paint and a splash of glitter.

Upper left: Beaded-tassel napkin rings have been rescued from the drawer and used to add an element of elegance to this tree.

Second from top: For an unusual seasonal tree ornament, a single-stemmed silk pansy was sprayed with adhesive and dipped in micro beads. A clip was attached to the back and the ornament was then clipped to the tree limb.

When turning the traditional into the gilded, a few items that look "expensive" can be added. Tree limbs can be tied with oversized bows of gold ribbon, and handmade ribbon-pin ornaments can be created to add a touch of opulence.

Too much of a good thing is simply wonderful.
—Liberace

45

Treasures dreamt of, wishes answered.
—Takashimaya

Copper and silver—nothing is more opulent than these precious metals, especially when combined for holiday decorating. This is Sara's house and for the holidays, she loves to decorate in the more avant-garde style using metallic colors and materials.

Among other decorations on her tree is a collection of silver ornaments I have given to her each Christmas from birth. Each is indicative of the year it was given—one is Ms. Piggy and was given the year the Muppets were introduced.

Sara and her husband Brett have started many of their own traditions that someday their children will learn to love and remember always.

Below: These stockings were made by Sara—her very first sewing project—using scraps of fabric, leftover buttons and beads, and a crazy-quilt technique.

Opposite and above: Sara purchased the copper trees on these pages, but they could be made by dipping copper threads in thinned white glue and wrapping them around a metal or foam base. A strand of Christmas lights inside the tree is magical.

In the homes of the rich and famous, even the animals are given handmade stockings of satin and velvet. We sell quilt books in the store to teach our customers how to make that which may be too extravagant to purchase!

Right: The bottom of the tree becomes a stage for collections and Christmas decor.

Traditionally, when we think of decorating the tree, we refer only to the branches and the top of the tree. The bottom of the tree is left untouched because it will eventually be covered with packages. However, for some families, the tradition is to place their packages in different areas of the room so that each recipient knows exactly which are theirs and where they are to be seated during the ceremony of "opening the packages." In this situation, the tree skirt can be of the finest design and materials because it will always be on view and the pieces that are placed on it become a new wonderland for family and guests alike to enjoy.

Decorating in a timber-lodge or Northwoods theme does not always bring to mind descriptive words such as rich and elegant—but it can. If the woodsy theme is likened to the hunts of the east with magnificent elk depicted in silver and crystal, heavy engraved silver hearts for the ladies, and heavily beaded "icicles," the image is far from one of log cabins and cute wooden bears.

One aspect of stylish decorating that we convey to our customers at *Ruby & Begonia* is that regardless of what your theme and style are, they can be combined to be exactly what you dream of for the gilded holiday you are about to celebrate. Northwoods can be elegant with the addition of silver, country can be Victorian by surrounding primitive wooden furniture and accessories with laces and fine linens, and traditional red and green can be glitzy by adding lots of glitter and glass. In this way, we teach to all who ask that it is always possible to turn ideas and inspiration into reality.

recapture a victorian *Christmas*

A Victorian Christmas was traditionally the season that was celebrated by both men and women. However, it was brought to its level of elegance, sophistication, and joy by the women in an era and a time that was less complicated and more gracious. It was in this Victorian time that hearth and home were decorated with great style; that gifts, regardless of how small, were specifically chosen for the receiver; and that entertaining was well planned and elaborate. It was an opportunity then, as it is now, to acknowledge friendships; to again feel the familiarity of traditional rituals—the stirring of the pudding, the decorating of the tree, the filling of the stockings; and to remember that wherever we are, it is during this season, that to home our hearts do travel.

At *Ruby & Begonia*, we try to offer a tiny touch of every style of Christmas. In the same way our designer, Penelope Hammons, tucks her tiny Victorian dolls and furniture under her staircase for little ones to discover and enjoy, we in the store add small touches of this most gracious of Christmas styles.

Above and right: Garlands of branches were stapled to the wood frame above one of the doorways in *Ruby & Begonia* and an abundance of frosted-glass pinecones were hung among the greenery. Some of the pinecones were tied with small tassels made from golden thread.

Far right: Vintage cards can be reproduced for sending to friends, reduced and placed in small frames hung from the tree, or pinned above doorways with other Christmas memorabilia (see above).

Opposite and right: Victorian-style terrariums can be used winter and summer to house fragile indoor plants or they can be used to create scenes of winter woodlands. In each of these, the bottom of the case was filled with glitter snow and then Christmas figurines and a variety of forest trees were added.

Below: A glass dome placed on a gold-leafed charger is a tabletop terrarium that has been redesigned to match the larger terrariums. The chargers we use have a variety of finishes. Some are large white serving plates, or sterling silver vegetable platters. Some we gold-leaf by hand, following easy manufacturer's directions.

Christmas for us is the returning to the gentle joys of the season. It is the re-creation of children caroling, of imagined angels in the snow, and of Santas that look more old and wise than fat and jolly. Each year as we unwrap the ornaments and unpack the trees to decorate both our homes and our shop, we carefully remove each piece of paper that protects our treasured decorations and recount our most precious memories. As some of our traditions endure and others are created, we continue to hold dear the memories filled with the joy and love of friends and family.

We do not remember days, we remember moments.
—Unknown

Above: Sara thinks that Victorian ornaments are often unacceptable because the faces appear to be a little too stern and severe. I, on the other hand, love their looks of all-knowing age and wisdom. Such ornaments, if vintage, can be rare and unaccessible. However, exact replicas can be made with collected pinecones from the yard, tiny bits of fleece and fur, and small pieces of felt. There are explicit directions in several books that can be purchased at needlework shops.

Bottom left: Small personalized tags can be inexpensive and quick to make and decorate—and more special than a card that is store-bought. These are simply price tags purchased from an office supply store.

Victorian-style decorating is often easier than a simpler more primitive style. Our designers and customers find it less complicated to add more and more to achieve the desired style than to get one single Santa to look just right on the mantel.

In the make-believe child-sized tea party to the right, linen doilies have been placed one on top of the other to create a tiny yet very elegant tablecloth. The small tree's metal stand was wrapped in a hand-stitched dish towel, and vintage toys and china were set for everyone.

Left: Fragile glass ornaments can be made more feminine by using the ornament as the base for a flower "arrangement."

Delicate silk roses, miniature glass balls, and beaded trim are what we use in the store to create elaborate Victorian style ornaments. Each ornament is designed in a color theme to accent the base. Each design component is a slightly different color so the arrangement exhibits uncommon depth and richness.

The delicate and intricate details of each ornament are what make Victorian decorating so extravagant. Each one represents an era when children and their mothers had time to sit and refine their handwork skills. This pin ornament, to the right, can be made so that several are exactly the same or so that each is completely different.

To make pin ornaments, simply create your designs using seed beads, sequins, small braids, and ¾" straight pins on a Styrofoam® form.

It is true that Christmas is for the young; however it is the adults who create the intricate decorations, prepare the elaborate meals, and record family memories. As we have grown into women, Sara and I have come to appreciate all Christmas has to offer. We love the faces of the children as they whisper to each other and wonder what might be inside each beautifully wrapped package. We love the way the trees look just before we turn the lights off at the end of the day; and we love each treasure that has been handmade and passed down from generation to generation.

Oftentimes, there is only one of these special treasured ornaments in a family's collection that can be handed down. When that is the case, we re-create the ornaments using techniques from our craft books.

Left: We sell these vintage replica ornaments which are reproduced from original Victorian Christmas decor. They can be re-created with glass beads, spools of craft wire, and thin silver chains.

Far center left: Tassels are an unexpected addition to the decorations on any Christmas tree. Traditionally used as curtain tiebacks or lamp pulls, they can double as a more ornate "icicle." Such tassels can be purchased or can be created by adding unusual finials to the top of store-bought plain tassels. Sections of the tassel can then have beads strung, be braided together, or have smaller tassels attached.

Left: Small garden ornaments can be brought in for the winter and used to adorn the holiday tree. In this way, such decorative items need not be stored, but can be enjoyed the year through.

One of the loveliest aspects of this time of year is that we are able to surround our-selves with beautiful things. We can make or purchase more items to display in our homes than is warranted during any other season of the year. This is the time for small unexpected surprises, a time when it is acceptable to combine the whimsical with the more elegant, and a time when it is appropriate to add one more decoration discovered long after the tree is completed.

Left: I love the angels, cherubs, and other figures that are used in the garden. This year, I carried in my heavy cement garden statues and used them to adorn my "forest" of trees. Because the statues will break and chip during the cold months of our climate, they must be stored away. They are too wonderful and too expensive to enjoy only three months out of the year, so I use them in my holiday decorating whenever I can.

Below: Fancy crystal light covers are one of my favorite ways to decorate a tree. They can serve two purposes: first, to add an additional glow to the tree, and second, to take the place of an ornament. When I began collecting light covers I was amazed at how many different types are available. Now I look for new ones everywhere I go.

Victorian ornaments are easily created with velvet leaves and flowers, beaded roses and butterflies, and large glass ornaments. One published designer, Mary Jo Hiney, made the ornament to the left by taking the glass piece of a discarded old table lamp and creating a bouquet of flowers on the top. She beaded the flowers, leaves, and the butterfly individually. If you do not wish to spend time beading, old pieces of jewelry can be used, beaded flowers can be purchased, and beaded leaves can be found in a florist shop.

This design idea can be adapted to any size for any occasion. Small replicas can be created on traditional glass ornaments, just make certain the glass ball is not too fragile to hold the bouquet. The arrangement can be a centerpiece if a glass vase is used as the base.

Right: Mary Jo also made this beaded rose ornament, which can also be re-created from old pieces of jewelry. What is worthy of notice here is the deep red beaded flower against the flocked white tree. It is an elegant statement that can be used to decorate an entire tree or as an accent on only one or two of the most prominent branches at eye level.

Heavenly Angels

Use the Cinnamon Dough Ornaments recipe on page 13. Roll out dough as instructed and cut out angel shapes. Transfer shapes to an ungreased cookie sheet. Bake as directed.

To decorate each angel, draw faces on watercolor paper and add details with colored pencils. Cut out faces and glue to angel-shaped cookies with craft glue. Using craft glue, attach beads and lace to decorate angels as desired; refer to photo at left. Attach yarn for hair. Make a loop with metallic cord for hanging and glue to the back of the angel.

Right: To make these vintage fruits, begin with plaster, papier-mâche, or plastic fruit shapes. Spray-paint them gold or silver, then roll in seed beads or use bead-head pins and push them in for an all-over design. Style in groups to arrange.

revisit a traditional
Christmas

Friends, family, and our customers who enjoy the trimmings of a traditional-style Christmas embrace the season's simplest rituals wholeheartedly. To them, celebrations of Christmas are important and the decorating is natural and designed in the colors of red and green for Christmas or blue and white for winter. The homes, both inside and out, of such traditionalists are decorated as if the decorations were the gifts they were giving to loved ones on Christmas morning.

All visitors who come to either the homes of these purists or to *Ruby & Begonia* are greeted with these traditional joys of the season. From the moment they enter the front walkway, a green wreath tied with a red velvet bow offers a merry welcome. As guests pass through the doors, they enter a realm where something seasonal rewards the senses at every turn—a fire in the fireplace, a pine-scented candle burning in the window, a favorite Christmas carol playing in the background, a tree in every room, Santas and candy canes and toy trains everywhere. These are the traditions that continue despite the changes that circumstance and time may bring.

Opposite: When creating our own wreaths, we use more than one species of evergreen. We try to incorporate several different types so each wreath offers an unexpected visual delight.

Right: Crystal star shapes that sparkle in the window are a simple addition that is a magical reminder of a season filled with hope and wonder.

Festive Painted Cloths

Stenciling white snowflakes on squares of sponged canvas can be used throughout the winter as place mats or for a table runner. To make this project, coat the design side of the canvas with gesso and let dry. Apply a solid coat of paint as a background then sponge-paint the entire cloth a lighter color; let dry. Dip a rubber stamp in a contrasting paint color and stamp images in any pattern you choose on the cloth. Re-apply paint on the rubber stamp as needed for clarity and color as pattern is applied. Let dry thoroughly. Coat painted side of fabric with 3–4 coats of matte varnish and let dry. Follow with 3–4 coats of matte varnish on the unpainted side of the fabric. Items may be wiped with a damp cloth but are not machine-washable.

63

Right: A traditional-style tree is decorated with things we have loved since we were children. These include nutcrackers, candy canes, toy drums, and multicolored lights and ornaments. The ornaments on overdecorated Christmas trees are wired to the outside of the tree's branches with thin yet strong florist wire. Thus the tree can be filled to overflowing with the magical symbols of the season.

Traditional decorations can be updated by taking what is expected and turning it upside down! This particular style of tree was introduced several years ago and is gaining in popularity. It is designed so that it appears to be upside down, which allows for more room at the bottom of the tree. It is also nice to have a tree with branches that are fuller at the top—in smaller rooms or in the shop—leaving valuable floor space unobstructed. One of our customers, designer Wendi Wolfard, simply could not agree to only a tree skirt for such a tree. She stacked boxes, presents, and toys under the tree and wired Santa so that he looked as if he were just about to deliver the entire "package" to a home filled with small children anxiously awaiting his arrival.

A traditional Christmas tree would not be complete without handmade ornaments, which have been collected since the children were young, and a toy train that really works.

Erecting a small town and toy train under and around the tree can become a family tradition remembered the whole year through. Small houses can be made during the summer months when the children are home from school. Life-like village additions in scale can be collected on vacations and used as decorations or given as gifts. After only a few years, the scene will resemble a giant scrapbook, holding the memories of more than just the days of Christmas.

Left: This tiny replica of an old steam engine entertains both young and old as they come to visit during the holidays.

Right: In traditional-style decorating, it is easy to have young children help make the ornaments. Gather together painted boxes and baskets, bags of hard candy, nuts, tiny ornaments, and miniature toys. Have the children fill the baskets with candy and toys and, when they are finished, glue the pieces together by pouring white glue over the contents. Let these dry thoroughly, then hang them on the tree's branches with bright-colored ribbons.

Left: Hard-candy decorations can be made as garlands by wrapping thin red ribbon around small white Styrofoam® balls. You can also tie the ends of wrapped candy together, which could be easier for young children. After the garlands are complete, swag them from tree branches and let them hang in bundles or bunches as if they were ornaments.

67

Christmas Block Garland
Paint a variety of purchased wooden beads with desired colors. Letters can be applied to individual beads, using rub-on decals or painted using store-bought stencils. String your beads on twine to spell out various festive phrases interspersed with plain-painted beads. Names of family members and pets can also personalize a tree.

Whether you present gifts in boxes or bottles, hang them on your tree or stack them among your gift packages, you will want to personalize each gift by creating some part or all of it by hand. Painting or stitching details, sewing on buttons, or tying on ribbons and bells says the receiver is worth that extra touch.

celebrate a new england
Christmas

Christmas in New England is as close to the first Christmas in the Colonies as one can get today. A blazing hearth is basic because it offers a feeling of warmth and security in this sparse style of home. Throughout New England style homes, Christmases are styled with simple decorations that are often primitive and natural. Strands of ruby-red cranberries are hung, as shown here from more than just the tree. Simple furniture is decorated with pine boughs and once-used items such as game boards act as accent pieces. The edible delights of the season are presented on ironstone pottery, transferware, pewter, or tinware. A freshly cut spruce tree is essential—for its fragrance as well as its historic appeal—and several are placed throughout a New England home. At the store, for such a Christmas vignette, we decorate our New England Christmas tree with carved wooden ornaments and pinecones. For many of our friends and family, this is their favorite Christmas style.

Upper left and below: A New England Christmas kitchen would not be complete without aromatic gingerbread cookies hanging in the window or garlands of dried fruit and bay leaves. A long wooden box on the windowsill can be filled with sprigs of greenery and the fruits of the season. Add red touches to each room in your home for festive cheer.

In our store, items are transformed from "everyday" to "holiday" with simple natural embellishments such as holly branches and bowls of fresh red berries. For us, this is the easiest style of Christmas for which to prepare, and oftentimes—because of its natural bounty and simplicity—the one enjoyed the most.

Early Christmases in the new world were celebrated by immigrants who brought family possessions to this new land. Even though they loved their new home, they treasured the memories of homes, families, and traditions that were left behind. Flags that they had once served, small replicas of thatched cottages where they had lived, and European Santas that they had believed in as children were all used as the decorations for the season. Because we live in Utah   a place where our ancestral heritage is studied by so many—we know several families who decorate their holiday homes with pieces that could have been carried here by their ancestors. These items are, for them, the link to those that came before.

73

Left: A tradition enjoyed by one of our close friends is that of collecting Santa Clauses. Because there are so many types and origins of Santas, she wants each of her children and grandchildren to know and love their history just as much as she does. As each large Santa is collected, a set of smaller similar Santas are purchased as well. Their histories are typed on scrolls, and a small Santa and scroll are given to each of the grandchildren on Christmas Eve.

Above: You need not own a New England style home to decorate for the holidays in typical New England fashion. Used in this region is a green wreath and one lighted candle in each window. The wreath offers passersby an eternal wish of good fortune for the holiday season, and the candle helps to light their way.

Right: Wreaths, pine boughs, and the fruits of the season are the welcome that is received by those who come to join in the celebrations of this family's Christmas. The swag above the framed portrait is one that has become associated with a Williamsburg style Christmas, yet fits perfectly with the natural decorations in this designer's contemporary New England style home.

It is appropriate for part of this designer's European style Santa collection to become the center of her holiday table decorations. When guests come for dinner, tiny wooden Santas are tied to homespun napkins with ribbon and a rosemary sprig, then placed on each pewter plate. When the meal is over, the dessert dishes have been cleared, and the guests prepare to leave, each is invited to take their Santa home to add to their own collection. It is a tradition that is looked forward to every year by family and friends. Each new season and each new Santa bring an evening filled with fond memories of good friends, good food, and good fun.

echo the northwoods this *Christmas*

A hardy Northwoods Christmas style relies heavily on combining the beauty of nature's seasonal bounty with the "stuff" of myth and legend. The Northwoods regions may be coastal or inland, but their decorating ideas will have elements in common. Pinecones and fir trees, acorns and autumn leaves bring old-world nostalgia to this rugged decorating style. In true Northwoods style, Santas are found in canoes and pinecones come in painted tin sap buckets. At our store, we accentuate the elements of the outdoors by using stars and bells of rusted tin for tree and table decorations and serve huge earthenware mugs of hot chocolate topped with marshmallows.

Northwoods decorating can include pieces that are not normally considered the "great outdoors" but in reality were and are. Vintage woodland Santas that were part of such local folklore and porcelain dolls that were played with by children who lived in such rugged country are wonderful collections to add to the more-masculine outdoor decorations. The collective display to the right could be left up the entire year. The items are what the designer loves and are more than just Christmas decorations.

Above: Dipping natural pinecones in colored wax is a quick way to achieve the candleholder and potted "trees."

Upper right: Floating pinecone candles can be placed in weathered metal containers and located throughout the house. When surrounded by pine boughs and pinecones, they look as though they were just brought in from outside.

Lower right: It is always nice to have trays of treats set out for hungry family members or unexpected guests. These crackers and nuts are served on a wooden tray and separated into small baskets that can be refilled often.

The Northwoods means camping, and camping means campfires, and campfires mean "s'mores."

We were delighted when we saw these wonderful little s'mores snowmen. They are made by threading a large quilting needle with twine, knotted at the end, through two marshmallows and tying off with a loop for hanging. Use a fine-tipped marker to make eyes, mouth, and buttons; the point of an orange toothpick for the "carrot" nose; twigs for arms and a miniature hat perched jauntily on top. Allow the pieces to harden overnight, then glue the snowman to the top of a piece of chocolate-brown felt glued on top of a real graham cracker square. Children and adults alike can help make these. Everyone loves them!

Left: Holiday decorating is one of the few times of the year that we can buy everything in one theme for the holiday season—decorations, decorative accessories, dishes and serving pieces—and everything should "go together." In the Northwoods Christmas corner at *Ruby & Begonia,* we set the table with Tracy Porter® dishes. The table coverings and napkins are matched to the dishes and, of course, the silverware handles can look like small twigs.

Left: Specialized Santas, such as this one from Lynn Haney, that appears to have walked straight from the Northwoods, may be difficult to find. However they can be created by purchasing a European style Santa and adding pieces of faux fur to the coat, a woven bag filled with splinters of wood, and undecorated miniature pine trees for him to carry. And don't forget the sled, canoe, or snowshoes for him to travel with through the woods.

Below: In Northwoods decorating, the gifts must match the theme. Packages can be given in decoupaged terra-cotta pots, presents can be wrapped in brown wrapping paper, or snacks can be served in tiny woven baskets.

We all love "things" that are little, like this dollhouse furniture of miniature beds, tiny chests, and flannel bedcoverings that are inspired by Ralph Lauren®. Two of our published designers, Terry Combe Johnson and Lael Combe Furgeson, created a series of miniature vignettes for *Ruby & Begonia* that can be used under a tree, in a dollhouse, or simply on the top of a table. This series was displayed at Christmastime when make-believe and ordinarily unessential decorative items are not only acceptable but required! Our patrons, both young and old, spent many afternoons inspecting the finest details of the fitted down comforters, the tiny knitted shawls, and the handcarved bear on the front of the chest. When making something this size, the magic comes from duplicating each detail of the actual life-sized item.

Backwoods Christmas Cabin

Cut bristol board for the walls and roof and glue or tape together. Trim the pretzels and glue to the house form as needed for the outside of the walls. For the roof, glue oyster crackers in rows to look like shingles. The chimney is simply four shredded-wheat biscuits glued together to form a square, then adhered onto the roof.

Apply snow texture sparingly to the roof, chimney, and house. Once dry, paint the windows and doors with brown acrylic paint. For an added touch of Christmas flair, add moss, berries, pinecones, or craft snow as desired.

Miniature delights need not be confined to furniture. Create a tiny village or cabin to enchant family members and holiday guests.

Right: Cabin-shaped baskets can be filled with goodies for guests who come to visit any Northwoods home. This "basket" was a purchased cabin with a removable roof. A hole in the top allowed it to be filled to overflowing with colorful toys and goodies. As the cabin's contents are enjoyed, the candy and cookies can be replenished.

relive a memorable
Christmas

The meanings of Christmases past are unique to each of us. When visitors come to our shop to share their treasured memories and show us their Christmas collections, we enjoy incorporating their traditions and ideas into the store displays. Elaborate hand-beaded ornaments, like the ones my grandmother used to make, are again popular and can be displayed from a more contemporary gold branch. On open shelves, windowsills, and fireplace mantels throughout *Ruby & Begonia*, we arrange miniature nativity scenes and crocheted villages of sugar-coated cottages and castles, sparkling trees, and tiny carolers. We enjoy re-creating the Christmases for which grandmothers and aunts spent hours decorating. It was a time of Barbie® dolls, poodle skirts, and mylar Christmas trees. It was splendid in its "kitschy" hand-made way.

Above: When I was a little girl, my grandmother would sit for hours and crochet small Christmas buildings out of fine white cotton crochet cord. She even taught me so that I could help her. When we were photographing for a magazine's Christmas article, I found this village in the home of Wendi Wolfard. Each tiny detail reminded me so much of my grandmother and winter afternoons in the early 1950s, that I found a retro crochet book and decided to try again that which my grandmother had shared and was a significant part of her holiday traditions.

Remembering is a dream that comes in waves.
—Helga Sandberg

Above left: Christmas decorations made from a collection of treetop finials are typical of elaborate but not necessarily expensive creations from designer Wendi Wolfard.

Above right: The beaded pin ornament is one Wendi made. She liked the ones she had seen in books and decided that she could make enough to fill her tree and then give each one to a friend.

The framed jewelry tree, to the right, is made from pieces collected by Wendi from her two sisters, her parents, grandparents, cousins, aunts, and friends. She arranged them, including her father's wedding cuff links and her and her sisters' prom necklaces and earrings, into this memory-filled and most wonderful retro symbol of the holidays.

Retro Jewelry Tree

A vintage jeweled Christmas tree can be made by spraying a piece of foam-core board with spray adhesive and covering the board with fabric, smoothing out the air bubbles with your hands.

Draw the outline of the tree on the fabric with chalk. Using a jewelry glue that dries clearly, adhere a string of beads to the chalk outline. Proceed to fill in the outline with jewelry, beads, and other jewel-like items.

Strands of beads can be glued on as garland and dangle earings used as ornaments on the tips of the branches. Let picture dry for 24 hours before framing.

89

Left: The hanging candleholders are created from the lids of several discarded coffee urns. Holes are drilled at several intervals, then beaded chains are added. Be careful not to use any flammable decorative filler.

Taken from the pages of our designer Binky Morgan's book, *Flea Market Jewelry*, this retro Christmas display is perfectly at home in her vintage clothing shop. Binky is an artist who loves old clothes and old shoes. When she realized she would need some new holiday decorations, she decided a fresh display of well-loved objects was the answer.

The small pair of beaded slippers, opposite page, were too sentimental to wear or to give away. Binky hung them on the wall, using two pierced earrings as push pins. This is a great idea whenever you want a fancy push pin to hang something.

Below: The blue package is made from cutting an evening dress, which was a vintage piece in her store, into smaller pieces of manageable wrap. The pin is a long-forgotten brooch that she found in a drawer.

Above: Ornaments are made as mementos by taking small vintage jewelry pieces, removing the backs, and adhering the pieces to glass Christmas balls.

Not all Christmas celebrations are decorated in red and green and some are far from traditional. Jill Dahlberg is a designer who loves pink and anything retro. Her design ideas and secrets inspired one of our customers to create the same holiday scene. One week before Christmas, she has an early holiday brunch for her closest women friends. Brunch is served buffet style and they gather together around her very '50s pink poodle tree to talk about the holidays, catch up on what has been missed, and plan their day. When brunch is complete, they climb into a hired limousine and spend the day shopping for last-minute Christmas gifts. It is a day of unusual extravagance as their driver drops them in front of their favorite stores, waits patiently for them to make their purchases, and then carries their packages to the car. It is a holiday experience that is looked forward to with much anticipation year after year.

Above and right: Collecting for and decorating a pink '50s buffet is as much fun as actually sharing the time with friends and family. In decor like this, almost anything pink and "kitschy" is acceptable. Plastic purses can hold paper plates, strands of inexpensive pink pearls can decorate vases of fresh roses, and plastic flatware can be served in something as unexpected as a toothbrush holder.

Left: Pink mylar Christmas trees are probably not traditional enough to be loved by all of the nieces and nephews in this designer's family, but they do love to come and see what she has done because she often lets them play with all of the little toys that she uses for decorating. These tiny poodles with jeweled collars can be wound up and released to bounce along the countertop. They are a favorite of young and old guests alike.

Below: Bring back childhood with a lollipop ice cream topper.

Opposite: A pink Barbie® doll gingerbread house—what could be more retro or more fun? Made for the fund raiser sponsored by a local bank (see page 16), it was the perfect addition to one of our designer's Christmas decorations. If you look very closely, you will see Barbie® dressed in her Christmas Eve best, stepping out to enjoy the holiday season.

Right: This is the back of Barbie's® house with her Volkswagon parked in the garage, ready for her to go to Grandmother's house.

Left: These place cards, or retro ornaments, can be made by painting big Christmas lights the desired color with acrylic paint. Using a small brush with white paint, letter a name, then wrap the bulb with one fuzzy pipe cleaner to use as a hanger.

May sweet content with you abide to bless your home at Christmastide.
—Unknown

create a natural
Christmas

Christmas is the highlight of the year for not only all of us at *Ruby & Begonia* but for many of our family and friends. For friends such as Jane Ream, who loves to garden, Christmas is all that is natural. Though the decorations are not created until the first weeks of December, they are planned for all year long. Bushes are planted in spring so that the berries they produce are available during the winter months; flowers are grown throughout the summer so they can be cut and dried for Christmas packages; leaves, acorns, and pinecones are gathered during crisp fall days

so they can be used with boughs of winter greenery. Gardeners love to create decorations with the plentiful ingredients from yard and greenhouse, which—when combined with well-loved decorations—begin to appear like evolving magical visions on doors, mantels, shelves, windowsills, and tabletops. Their compositions change from year to year, sometimes even week to week. Their colors are both deep and muted; their scents are of fresh flowers, pine boughs, and spices. Their appeal is timeless—bound by no season or celebration.

Left: Decorating naturally can oftentimes go from the simple to the overdone in the twinkling of an eye. If the snowfall is less than average, or if you live where there is no snowfall, the dreary browns of a winter landscape can sometimes become overwhelming. Decorating the inside of your home—and our shop—this time of year means an abundance of fresh greenery, blooming winter bulbs, and poinsettias to lift spirits. It makes winter seem as bountiful and fresh as a garden in spring.

Roses are always a welcome addition to any holiday decoration in any style; but they are especially appreciated in the winter months when the sight of roses in bloom may not be as common as during the months of summer. This bouquet of roses was placed in a sterling silver salad bowl, which was then placed on a vanity mirror to increase the impact of such a beautiful piece. The color of the roses was selected because the soft yellow accentuates the crystal rather than overpowering it as dark red roses might. The yellow helps to highlight the gold accents on the table. Remember, Christmas need not always be red and green, pinecones, and pine boughs.

For one of our designers, decorating naturally is taken more literally than it is for some. In place of ornaments on her tree, tiny bundles of lavender are tied and the animals that she raises on her farm are duplicated in her decor. Notice, too, the border of natural pine boughs that surround her room and are left unadorned as if they were simply growing there. Her packages are wrapped in natural brown paper so as not to detract, even for a moment, from the natural beauty of the tree.

Oversized amaryllis should be displayed in every natural Christmas decor and should be given a place of prominence. In designer Jane Ream's home, a beautiful display is placed in the entry just inside the front door as a welcome to her family and friends. Rather than putting such pieces on the tabletop or floor, she places them on a small pedestal next to a favorite Christmas painting or print on an easel.

Above: Pomander balls are familiar to all of us who probably helped make them for holiday decorations when we were children. Regardless of how familiar we are with them, they are always welcome. These pomanders have been completed in different styles. Some are covered completely with cloves and some are only partially decorated in spirals or stripes. Fresh oranges in the bottom of the bowl add color and the sprigs of pine boughs add a scent and texture of their own.

Above: A favorite recipe served at *Ruby & Begonia* is the addition of caramel syrup to heated apple juice. You will want to use juice because cider is too strong in flavor. When cinnamon sticks are added, your guests will be delighted at the flavor of caramel apples with a hint of something unexpected.

Decorating in a natural style can be the use of fresh greens, but it can also be the incorporation of dried fruits, vegetables, and flowers that may have been purchased or may have been grown in your garden. Natural is also the selection of colors and materials. Natural colors are those that can be obtained from natural dyes such as cranberries or tea-staining, and the materials are always 100% natural cotton or wool.

101

Love is a canvas furnished by nature and embroidered by imagination.
—Voltaire

Decorating naturally can make a bold statement that is extravagant in nature. It may be easy and fairly inexpensive or a lavish investment, as in these photos, to add an abundance of greenery and fresh flowers to every area of your home. Poinsettias are readily available this time of year and are often much more reasonably priced than large Santas or ceramic figurines. It is true that natural decorating must be replaced every year; however, one advantage is that they do not have to be stored. At *Ruby & Begonia*, we add as many natural elements in an overstated manner as we can. They are so beautiful when lights are added and all is aglow during the long evening hours. Porcelain figurines or other "unnatural" decor do not elicit the same response as when a friend or customer first experiences the beautiful sights and scents of a natural Christmas.

Right: This beautiful Christmas tree has been decorated with sprigs of raffia, sprays of artificial red berries, pinecones, and a collection of nativities in miniature moss-covered stables. In keeping with the natural tone of the decor, grapevine garland was wound about the tree. To continue the theme beyond the tree, display a larger nativity on the floor beneath. The simplicity of this natural design expresses the serenity, peacefulness, and spirituality of the season.

Packages can become dramatic presentations to the recipient with the addition of lavish natural touches. Gilded pinecones, luxurious or sheer net ribbons, or a beaded garland in complementary natural colors all add an elegant touch to an otherwise understated look.

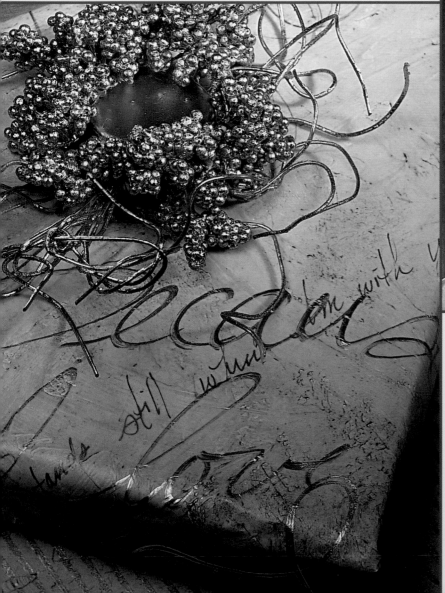

Left: Dried natural materials can be gilded by using gold spray or dipping in gold metallic paint. Simple craft papers can be embellished with a small wreath of golden pepper berries or other materials in place of a bow as a finishing touch for a more formal nature-inspired gift.

select a theme this *Christmas*

In November, when the holidays are just around the corner, each of us begins to seriously think about Christmas. At *Ruby & Begonia*, we sit down, look at the calendar, and try to realistically plan when the trees should be purchased, when the ornaments should be gently unwrapped, when the decorations should be put on display, in addition to when the parties should be held and what should be served. Most of us will use the same decorations that we used the year before, and the year before that. Due to the expense of new decorations and the limits on storage space that most of us contend with, reusing what we have is the only rational choice we can make. At *Ruby & Begonia*, we teach our customers how to take what exists, select a different "theme" for this year's decorations, and make the two work together with a minimal amount of new investment in time, money, or space.

New theme ideas are endless. In the store, we are inspired by such concepts as fairy tales and stories, retro, film making, sports, pets, or gourmet cooking. We take the expected and "magically" help to create the unexpected.

Wizards and witches, hobbits and nymphs, woodland creatures both great and small are what we see wherever we might look due to the popularity of *Harry Potter* and *The Lord of the Rings*.

Literary works of art and cinematography masterpieces are magical and could be included in every year's decor. Not everyone will want the bright colors and distinctive features of these little creatures in their Christmas decorations; but for those who believe in magic and make-believe, they can be easily incorporated into existing traditional decor.

Red, green, and gold are often-used Christmas colors as well as the major colors of such creatures. All one need add is a touch of purple, a few twigs, some moss, and a creature or two and you will have created a wonderland of wizardry, enchantment, and mystery. If you are a seamstress, work with clay; or are a dollmaker, it will be a year for creating your own small fairy folk. Inexpensive elves and nymphs can be purchased and embellished with bits of fabric, beads, tassels, small pieces of jewelry, and other treasures. This was the tree that I loved most this year; and who can imagine what it will be next year.

107

Our friend Sheila Jones decorated a winter garden tree for the Christmas Tree Jubilee, the annual Weber County School District Foundation fund raiser that benefits special-needs children. She styled it in the lavish colors of painted jeweled butterflies, velvet green poinsettias, yards of ribbon resembling green vines in the branches of the tree, and tiny red lights appearing to be winter berries. She hung gold tassels, sprigs of berries, and leaves sprayed gold. Sheila made certain that the details realistically represented the ways of the garden, placing sprayed limbs to look as if they were "growing" from the trunk of the tree. If you create such a tree, position butterflies to appear as if in flight, and wind the ribbons down through the branches. This is a wonderful, very fanciful tree that brings the beauty of the garden into any Christmas celebration.

Each Christmas, I create a "forest" of trees in my living room and we select a new theme that is different from the previous year. This year my husband asked that everything on our trees be white or silver. He did not want the trees to be flocked as we usually do, and he wished for a star on top of each one. We created a variety of long drooping garlands and combined them with crystal and silver ornaments, many resembling delicate snowflakes. Our Christmas forest is a long-time tradition for Sara, my son Justin, and me, as is changing the theme each year. The unexpected is what we expect.

These pictures of my home during the holidays have appeared in two of Chapelle's publications. Thus, because it is so "me," a book on Christmas style written partially by me would be incomplete without them. Extravagant decorating is often used to celebrate a very special event, which is just what the year of my 50th birthday was for me. Because I so hated turning 40 and I was so determined to "love" turning 50, I celebrated for my entire 50th year. There were parties of every style, presents always, and gourmet food whenever I wished. To end such a year of celebrating, Christmas had to be magnificent and a little "over-the-top." During a trip with Sara, we purchased a vintage satin ball gown, which I decorated as one of my Christmas trees. Birthday cake with blue frosting and white roses was served to my annual holiday party guests, all of whom made my growing older a time filled with memories I shall cherish forever. I have already begun to plan for the year I turn 60 and what a celebration it will be!

Sara's favorite fairy tale, for as long as I can remember, has been Cinderella. So one year we decided to make her most-loved story our Christmas theme. One tree was left natural and decorated with the lovable objects that surrounded Cinderella while she lived with her wicked stepmother and evil stepsisters. When Sara's friends would come to visit, they would see the brooms Cinderella swept with, the mice and tiny birds that kept her company, the moon and stars she wished upon, and the pumpkins that were to become so important. Everyone's favorite, however, were the wicked stepsisters and their mother. These wonderful cloth dolls were designed and created by internationally acclaimed artisan Julie McCullough.

The base of the tree was surrounded by gift packages wrapped with brown kraft paper and tied with string. There were baskets of pumpkins, apples, and oranges; stick bundles; and stuffed teddy bears that were Cinderella's secret friends.

The second tree was blanketed in a layer of snow and stardust glitter and decorated for Cinderella at the ball. The ornaments were Cinderella's glass slippers on delicate blue velvet cushions, the lights were wedding bells with tiny birds attached, and there were Cinderella's coach ornaments on the branches. The tree was strung with glass beads and watched over by Cinderella's fairy Godmother, whose place of distinction was, of course, the top of the tree.

The packages under the tree were placed on a layered lace tree skirt that could have been Cinderella's petticoat, and were wrapped in the invitations to the ball.

On the mantel where the stockings are hung was my collection of crystal candlesticks. My dear friend, Linda Durbano, gives me a new one each year for Christmas and they are always the center of my holiday decorating. However, the "coaches" were my favorite. They were made from plastic Halloween pumpkins in which children might carry their candy.

Anita Louise Crane, a Chapelle designer, loves to decorate for the holidays with seashells. Even though she lives in the mountains of Park City, Utah, the treasures shared by the sea are some of those that are dearest to her heart. On her tree, you will find large white starfish, porcelain-shell angels created by Margaret Furlong, as well as scallop shells that have had a small hole drilled in them and are hung from ribbon.

Anita wraps her packages in white paper on which she has rubber-stamped delicate shell designs, then ties tiny shells with raffia to adorn them.

Opposite center: Small shells were glued to a papier-mâché cone base to create this tabletop tree. One type of shell or a variety of shell styles can be used.

Opposite left: Anita created the string of lights on her tree by gluing two clamshells together over large Christmas lights on a cord. If you make a set of your own lights, make certain that you use a silicone glue to connect the two clamshells. When the lights become warm, other glues tend to soften and the clamshells will separate and fall to the floor.

Above: The base of this seashell wreath is a grapevine wreath to which sprigs of eucalyptus, pinecones, clamshells, pomegranates, and other natural items have been added.

Left: Christmas gifts for those who love the sea could be apothecary jars filled with scented bath salts. Use as scoops the shells that have been collected along the beach.

A whimsical Christmas, filled with everything sweet, was created by one of the employees at *Ruby & Begonia* for her small grandchildren. She hung large glass candy pieces from her chandelier over the dining-room table. The children were served slush from a lighted bowl filled with flavored shaved ice that looked like old-fashioned rock candy. A tabletop "candy" tree was created by adhering even rows of small pieces of candy to a foam base. The family Christmas tree was decorated with candy canes, old-fashioned lollipops, and garlands created by stringing pieces of hard candy.

Left: With a whimsical theme for Christmas, a small number of very fanciful ornaments and decorations must be included. Here is a green bird with very long legs wearing a Santa hat. He was purchased; but if one could not be found to buy, such a delight can be easily created. At the toy store, buy a very strange stuffed animal that you think is appropriate and decorate it with feathers, small ornaments, and other Christmas decorations.

117

Kevin Dilley, one of my photographers, and I were invited to photograph the trees at the Christmas Tree Jubilee. A local film buff decorated one of the trees with all that has to do with the "movies." An old-fashioned film reel was used as the tree topper, bows were made from exposed rolls of film, a director's clapboard was included, and boxes of theater candy and popcorn became the ornaments. Even the wrapping for the packages had to do with going to the movies.

This is a wonderful example of how your family's passion can become part of your seasonal decorating. It may not be a tree that you want to use every year; but in a year when something special occurs, Christmas is a perfect time to remember.

Left: Exposed rolls of film were used to make "ribbon" bows and secured to the tree with florist's wire.

Below: Clear-glass hanging ornaments were filled with popcorn and hung from the tree. Another option would be to use cardboard theater popcorn boxes, available at craft and super discount chain stores.

To control the costs of theme trees such as this one, items used to decorate the tree can also be gifts for family and friends. On Christmas morning, family members can look for the tags that indicate which decorations on the tree are theirs. Boxes of candy can be for children, videos and DVDs can be given to everyone, theater tickets can be included in boxes of popcorn. The film canister could even hold the tickets and information for a family vacation to Universal Studios.

My husband, Michael, is a sport's enthusiast—with baseball being his biggest passion. He decorates his sports-room Christmas tree with the items from the wide world of sports that bring him joy.

His tree is flocked white and has red lights. The branches are decorated with ornaments detailed to represent a wide variety of his favorite sports, including basketball, baseball, football, soccer, and tennis. The tree is accented between the sports balls with simple red and silver glass ornaments.

Opposite center and right: Michael's sports ornament collection is extensive and a source of delight for all of the men in our family as well as those who visit our home during the holidays.

Wherever in the country Michael and I travel, we usually find the time to enjoy a "game" of some kind. While at stadiums, arenas, or ballparks, he buys a memento that could be used as an ornament on his tree. He is always on the lookout for Santas or nutcrackers that are dressed in team uniforms.

Left: This advent calendar was given to Sara's "Grammy Buehler" by her grandchildren, who filled the compartments with surprises. I loved it so much that it is the inspiration for next year's sport's calendar from me to my husband Michael.

My plan for Michael's sport's advent calendar is that each day when he opens a door he will find a note from me or a small gift that has to do with sports. Some gifts will be tickets to a local game, some will be tiny ornaments for his tree, and on the 25th he will find one of his Christmas gifts, which will be a trip to a major sporting event somewhere that he would like to see.

121

September 11, 2001, had an enormous impact on so many people in so many places around the world. For me, it was something that should never be forgotten. The following Christmas, I decorated our forest of trees in our patriotic colors. I chose not to include American flags; but it was important to me to celebrate the spirit, the ideals, and the strength of our red, white, and blue. The seven trees in the center of the room were left white while the two sets of three trees on either end of the living room were decorated so that one tree in each setting was one complete color. The ornaments were not "American" in theme, the colors were enough to express what I wanted to say.

Above: Each tree included stars that were made in the colors of the tree on which they were hung. It was important to me that the stars be included, because they are so representative of so many ideals for not only the Christmas season but for the everyday lives that we all live.

Right: When my trees are not large enough to set on the floor, I will often set them on pedestals in big pots that I bring in from the garden shed. I like the idea that not all of the trees are the same size and of the same type. I buy three or four different "real" pine trees to place in front of the artificial trees. In this way, my guests can smell the fresh trees and even tend to think all of the trees are fresh.

rekindle a hearthside *Christmas*

The heart of any Christmas celebration is the home, and for many, the heart of the home is that room in the house where the fire blazes and the family gathers to share the joys and traditions of the holiday season.

At holiday time, many of the trimmings for a place of such honor are chosen from natural materials, the bounty of the harvest, and of course, fresh-cut greenery which is symbolic of everlasting life. Sometimes family collections are added; but whatever the composition, the seasonal display must be one that is worthy of adoration. At *Ruby & Begonia,* we have a tiny fireplace in one corner of the shop and during the holidays we change the mantel almost weekly because there are simply too many ideas to share with customers and friends.

Above: A massive fireplace with heavy stonework is a perfect backdrop for a magnificent oversized Christmas display. What is unusual about this designer's mantel decor is the way that the wreath is connected by garlands to the arrangement on the mantel. The garland does not have lights attached, but the gold balls placed throughout the pine boughs and in the large glass jars catch the reflection from the light in the fireplace and fill the entire room with a golden glow.

The warm sense of hearth and home is reinforced when the tree or hearth is decorated with family keepsakes. A tradition practiced by our friend Jane Ream, is to place her family's collection of vintage dolls on the tree. She includes fresh roses in vials of water attached to the tree but hidden in the branches. The roses are unusually beautiful and add their fragrance to the pine boughs. A lovely touch of the outdoors is brought inside to remind us of the rebirth that will occur in the garden outside.

Large fireplaces in great rooms are ideal for adorning with enormous decorations. Because the pieces used are oftentimes expensive, one designer's secret is to keep the decor items on the mantel that are there throughout the year and add to them. On the mantel's center, she places a Christmas piece as a focal point, such as the deer on the mantel above. On either end of the mantel, the candlesticks that are the year-round decor are arranged, and she then surrounds them all with fresh pine boughs. On the hearth, bundles of dried rosemary are placed so that each evening they can be tossed on a blazing fire to release their rich aroma. Decorations in rooms where family and friends gather can be as simple or ornate as you wish. However, make certain they do not block walkways or make the room uncomfortable in any way for those who visit.

A hearthside Christmas celebrates personal yuletide traditions that are remembered by individual families all across America. One such family tradition is to have decorations filled with holly and ivy, pinecones and candles, oranges and apples, blue spruce and piñon pine, all carefully arranged on the mantel where on Christmas Eve stockings will be hung. This family waits to bring in the tree until Christmas Eve when everyone is together. After dinner is served, the towering tree is decorated by everyone gathering around and taking turns retelling their favorite Christmas story. As each story is told, a new ornament—a gift from the storyteller—is placed on the tree. After the stories are told, the packages are opened and dessert is served. The ornaments from years past are placed on the branches of the tree by everyone. This tradition is for a family whose days before the holidays are so busy that the decorating of the tree is a chore.

127

Hessian soldiers fighting for the British in the Revolutionary War were the first to introduce Christmas trees to this country. At that time, however, they were small tabletop-sized trees that were usually placed by the hearth in early-American homes. It was not until the mid-nineteenth century that the wondrous floor-to-ceiling Christmas tree that we are so fond of today became popular. Today, when creating a hearth-side style of decorating, you will often find many sizes of trees because they play such an important role in Christmas festivities. Smaller trees are a perfect back-drop or accent for collections of Santas, for creating small villages, for fireplace mantels, or to place on table-tops with small gifts for unexpected guests who may come to call. The larger trees are now the ones that are placed beside the hearth.

Now join your hands, and with your hands your hearts.
—William Shakespeare

When helping our clients to design mantelpiece displays for their own homes, we often tell them secrets we have learned from our designers. Use three focal points, the main point of interest in the center and one on either side, which become secondary focal points. The center can be a Christmas picture that is framed and set on the mantel or a large wreath like the one shown below. The two secondary points of interest can be candelabrum, tabletop-sized trees, or large standing Santas. The greenery that is put on the mantel should be of more than one type and designed in sprays of different heights so the arrangement on the mantelpiece does not appear too flat. If candles are placed among the greenery, make certain they are contained as a safety precaution. As greens become dry and brittle they are an extreme fire hazard. Replace them as necessary.

come home for
Christmas

When family and friends are reunited for the Christmas holidays, the entrance to a home should establish the warm, welcoming spirit of being together again. As we decorate *Ruby & Begonia* for the holidays, from the sidewalk to the shop doors to the holiday scenes inside, our goal is to welcome the family and friends who visit.

You too can hint at surprises to come, then fulfill them with personal touches. Walkways outlined with twinkling lights, luminaries on the steps, and potted poinsettias on stairways greet holiday guests. Once they are inside, sparkling trees and wreaths, European Santas and angelic figurines, candlelight and Christmas dinner enhance the celebration. Gifts opened on Christmas Eve by young children who cannot wait, stories of holidays past told by the fire, and carols sung around the tree are all part of the memories guests will take with them when they leave. These are why the home is the heart of Christmas.

Above: Collecting Christmas decorations can become very expensive, so one idea that we promote in the store is to encourage our customers to buy one very nice collectible decoration each year. It is amazing how quickly the years pass and their enviable collections grow. This is the time that larger decor items like the life-sized Santa or one of the vintage dolls can be purchased. In our family's case, each year I give Sara and her husband Brett, as well as Justin and his girlfriend Adie, one very beautiful Santa who always has a silver ornament with the date engraved hanging somewhere from his arm or his pack. Not only is this a way to expand a collection, but the giving of the Santa has become a wonderful tradition that is looked forward to with anticipation in our family.

One of our friends, Kathy Goddard, loves the holidays and decorates her home in every corner to welcome family and friends to their annual Christmas party. She uses beautiful lighted garlands and heavily woven tassels around her mirrors. The delicate glass ornaments are hand-blown and are souvenirs she collected while she and her husband Kelly were traveling. Kathy wants to help make her family and friends feel very special and one way this is accomplished is to attend to every detail such as with the staircase newel post below. All of her staircases are wrapped in garlands so that as you go from area to area you feel you are in a forested wonderland.

Right: In our friend Jane Ream's house, she uses lighted garlands to encircle her guests in a forested wonderland. In her dining room, the garlands are subtly attached to the wooden molding.

One way to attach garlands to molding is to place tiny nails with large round heads in the wood right where the trim meets the ceiling. Wrap a very thin, but strong, florist wire around sections of the garland and tie the wire to the nail. When both the garland and the nails are removed, there is no evidence that elaborate holiday decorations were there. It is also the method used to attach the beautifully decorated cascades of pine boughs between her windows.

Unusual Santas, vintage glass ornaments, large pots of fresh poinsettias, and oversized baskets under the tree, filled with everything from presents to pinecones, are items that will intrigue family and friends and brighten the holidays, year after year.

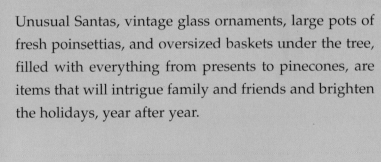

135

Opposite: In addition to the beautiful garlands that adorn the top of the large furniture pieces in this customer's home, she hangs enormous kissing balls in all of the rooms. The balls are decorated with pine boughs, ribbons, tassels, and mistletoe.

Left and above: At *Ruby & Begonia* we create gift baskets in our most unusual gift basket store *The White Fig*.

Personalized gift baskets are a nice idea for customers who have holiday guests from out-of-town. The gift baskets, which are created to match the Christmas decor, can be given to guests the night they arrive to make their stay even more special. If they have driven to be with friends and family during the holidays, the baskets filled with edible treats can be given to them to be enjoyed on their return trip home.

Sara and I love Christmas and all of the traditions that are relived and remembered each year during this wonderful season. We hope that we have given you ideas to add a touch of sparkle to your holiday decorating, and suggestions for creating new traditions to be shared with family and friends. Most of all, we hope we have helped you to create ideas of your own that will become part of your most memorable holiday celebrations. Thank you for sharing a very special season with us.

May the special moments of today be the most remembered memories of tomorrow.

—Unknown

139

About the Authors

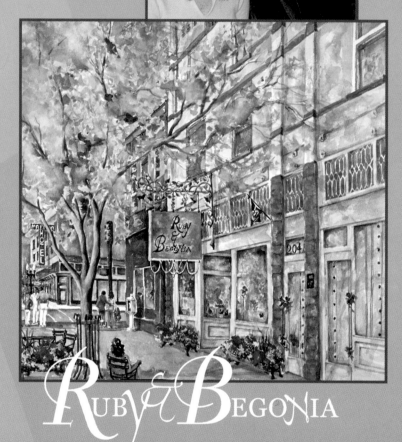

Jo Packham is President of Chapelle, Ltd., a 25 year-old publishing company that co-publishes books solely for Sterling Publishing which is now owned by Barnes and Noble. Sara Toliver, Jo's daughter, joined the Chapelle staff in 2000 as Vice President. A recent MBA graduate, she is the company's marketing/advertising director and oversees all managerial and financial aspects of their retail establishments.

On September 14, 2001, Sara and Jo opened *Ruby & Begonia*, a retail gift and home decor establishment which is, as their logo implies, "an embarrassment of riches." At *Ruby & Begonia*, both the inventory and the permanent display pieces are considered imaginative works of art. The inventory in *Ruby & Begonia* changes with the first day of each new month, offering the customer completely new products and displays for decorating ideas. In addition to retail sales, *Ruby & Begonia* is used as the photography studio and prop supply for the 60 hardbound books Chapelle does per year.

In August of 2002, *Ruby & Begonia* received the Gold Award for excellence in Visual Merchandising, top honor in their division for the 51st annual award presentation of *Gifts and Decorative Accessories* magazine.

In October of 2002, Sara and Jo opened a second store, *The White Fig*, which is "a most unusual gift basket company." In September of 2003 a garden store will be added to their retail establishments, as will a French bakery and a complete stationery store in the following two years.

Mother and daughter, publishing company, authors, retail stores . . . a story worth telling. Jo Packham and Sara Toliver are a mother-daughter team who have a story of growing up and going into business together; of failure and success; of imagination, commitment, endurance, and hope.

A Special Thank You

Sara and Jo extend a special thank you to their friends and customers who so generously shared their homes and holiday decorating ideas.

Dixie Barber
Holly & Joe Bauman
Eleanor "Grammy" Buehler
Anita Louise Crane
Jill Dahlberg
Linda Durbano
Lael Combe Furgeson
Kathy & Kelly Goddard
Penelope Hammons
Mary Jo Hiney

Terry Combe Johnson
Sheila Jones
Julie McCullough
Binky Morgan
Jane Ream
Wendi Wolfard

Thanks also to the Weber County School District Foundation's Christmas

Tree Jubilee for special-needs children, and to the Bank of Utah and their gingerbread house display, benefiting Christmas Box House and the Catholic Community Services Food Bank. We appreciate their cooperation in allowing us to photograph their holiday creations.

Metric Conversion

mm-millimetres   cm-centimetres
inches to millimetres and centimetres

inches	mm	cm	inches	cm	inches	cm
1/8	3	0.3	9	22.9	30	76.2
1/4	6	0.6	10	25.4	31	78.7
1/2	13	1.3	12	30.5	33	83.8
5/8	16	1.6	13	33.0	34	86.4
3/4	19	1.9	14	35.6	35	88.9
7/8	22	2.2	15	38.1	36	91.4
1	25	2.5	16	40.6	37	94.0
1 1/4	32	3.2	17	43.2	38	96.5
1 1/2	38	3.8	18	45.7	39	99.1
1 3/4	44	4.4	19	48.3	40	101.6
2	51	5.1	20	50.8	41	104.1
2 1/2	64	6.4	21	53.3	42	106.7
3	76	7.6	22	55.9	43	109.2
3 1/2	89	8.9	23	58.4	44	111.8
4	102	10.2	24	61.0	45	114.3
4 1/2	114	11.4	25	63.5	46	116.8
5	127	12.7	26	66.0	47	119.4
6	152	15.2	27	68.6	48	121.9
7	178	17.8	28	71.1	49	124.5
8	203	20.3	29	73.7	50	127.0

Acknowledgments

The publishers wish to thank the following for use of their products:

Barreveld Int.
3027 Route 9
Cold Spring, NY 10516
Barreveld candlesticks p. 44

Bethany Lowe Designs
16655 County Hwy. 16
Osco, IL 61274
www.bethanylowe.com
Crescent moon p. 51

Blessings Bowl
Alchemy IV, L.L.C.
4201 Mathews Way
Salt Lake City, UT 84124
Blessings bowl p. 29

Dept. 56
One Village Place
6436 City West Parkway
Eden Prairie, MN 55344
Three Wisemen pp. 40–41

Ercole Inc.
10 Jay Street Floor 8
Brooklyn, NY 11201
ercoleinc@aol.com
Mosaic stemmed vases p. 43

Margaret Furlong
Life Journey Keepsakes
Salem, OR
Shell angels p. 114

H. Potter
P.O. Box 6144
Lincoln, NE 68506
www.Kammiehpotter.com
Contact: Kammie Renter
Terrarium pp. 52–53

Hessel Studios
134 Paul Dr. #9
San Rafael, CA 94903
www.Hesselstudios.com
Copper candlesticks p. 22

Jim Marvin
Box 611
160 South Mulberry St.
Dickson, TN 37055
Glass pinecone ornaments p. 51

Lynn Haney
3515 34th Street
Lubbock, TX 79410-2831
Santa pp. 45, 78, 83

Mark Roberts
2501 West 5th St.
Santa Ana, CA 92703-1816
www.mark-roberts.com
Santa on a yak p. 135

Still Life
147 Golden Hind Passage
Corte Madera, CA 94925
realleaves@earthlink.net
Leaf & nutshell ornaments p. 28

Tracy Porter
⅝ Zrike Company Inc.
8 Thornton Rd.
Oakland, NJ 07436
Bear with bowl p. 82

Barbie® pp. 86, 94–95

Mary Engelbreit® p. 36

Ralph Lauren® p. 85

Space would not permit the inclusion of every vendor item photographed for this book, nor could all of them be identified. Inquiries may be made by calling Ruby & Begonia at 801-334-7829 or on the web site. www.rubyandbegonia.com

Photography

Kevin Dilley for Hazen Photography
14, 16–17, 21(UL), 22(L), 23, 26, 28–29, 31(L)(UR), 32(R), 33(UR)(LR), 34(UR), 35–36, 37(L)(UR), 44(L), 45(UL)(LL)(2nd to LL), 46–50, 51(U)(LL), 52–53, 54(UL)(2nd to LL)(UR), 57(L), 58–60, 61(LR), 69(MR), 79, 82(UR), 93(L), 94, 95(L), 104, 108–109, 110(LL), 118(R), 119, 122–124, 131–134, 135(LL), 136(L)

Jim Frankoski
98, 99(LR), 100, 126(LL), 135(UR), 136(LR)

Leslie Newman
8

Michael Skarsten
1–5, 6(UL)(R), 7, 45(2nd to UL)(UR), 64, 67(LL)(UR), 68(ML), 102–103, 106–107, 133(LR)

Jessie Walker
10, 11(LR), 70–72, 73(UR), 74, 75(L), 76–77, 96–97, 99(L)

Scot Zimmerman
12(R), 18–20, 21(UR), 34(UL), 40–42, 43(UR), 55, 56(LR), 65(R), 66(L), 68(UL), 69(LR), 73(L), 75(UR), 78, 82(LL), 83(L), 86(L), 87–88, 89(L), 116–117, 120–121, 125, 126(UR), 127–130, 133(T), 135(LR), 137–139

Comstock, Inc. © 2001
25, 30, 44(UR), 57(UR), 62, 89(LR), 101(UL)

Corbis Corp. © 1999
38(LR)

Photodisc, Inc. © 1993, 1996, 1999, 2000
9(UL)(UR), 12(LL), 38(LR), 51(LR), 54(2nd to UL)(LL), 56(UL), 63(LL), 65(LL), 66(LR), 68(LL), 86(LR), 99(UR), 101(R), 118(UL)

Index